GET TO THESE GOOD FRIENDS!

It's good to have friends who can help you. The saints are those kinds of friends! They help us by showing us ways to live as Jesus lived. Some saints did heroic things. Others lived more quietly. Every saint was different, but no saint was perfect.* When they made mistakes, they came to Jesus, said they were sorry, and tried again. Saints show us that even though we sin, Jesus will forgive us and help us do better, as long as we ask.

Some saints lived long ago. Others lived more recently. But today, they all live in heaven with Jesus, in perfect joy and peace. That's another way saints help us—they can bring our prayers right to Jesus!

You're friends with Jesus too, right? That means you can be a saint! Learn about some saints here. Try the activities, and have fun—with your friends, the saints!

✱ ACTUALLY, ONE SAINT is PERFECT.
Do you know who? (Hint: you can read about her on the next page!)

TWENTY-THIRD PUBLICATIONS *A division of Bayard, Inc.*
One Montauk Avenue, Suite 200 • New London, CT 06320 • (860) 437-3012 or (800) 321-0411
www.twentythirdpublications.com

Copyright © 2019 Connie Clark. All rights reserved. No part of this publication may be reproduced in any manner without prior written permission of the publisher. Write to the Permissions Editor.

ISBN: 978-1-62785-459-7 • Images: ©Shutterstock.com • Printed in the U.S.A.

MARY

JANUARY 1

Our greatest saint gives us our greatest gift!

Friends sometimes give each other gifts. Mary gave us the greatest gift. Here's what happened: An angel visited and told Mary that God had chosen her to be the mother of his Son. Mary could have said she wasn't ready, or that she was too busy. Instead, Mary said, "May it be done to me according to your word." Mary said yes to God's call (even though she didn't understand it completely).

> **GOOD QUESTION!**
> Is God asking you to do something? How can you say yes, the way Mary did?

When Mary said yes, she helped give us God's Son Jesus—our first and greatest Christmas present! But Mary wasn't finished giving gifts. She said yes to God all her life. When she learned that her older cousin Elizabeth was going to have a baby, Mary went to help her. When Joseph had to make a long trip to Bethlehem, Mary came with him, even though she was about to give birth to baby Jesus. When Jesus suffered on the cross, he asked Mary to be a mom to his friend John, and to all people. And Mary is the mother of us all, to this day! Mary is also the Queen of the Saints—that's why we put her first!

Plan a Party for Mary!

Color the picture of Mary. Then draw decorations all around her for a party. Add flowers, hearts, a picture of you, a prayer, or whatever you think Mary would like on her feast day.

GOOD to KNOW

A **FEAST DAY** is a time to remember and celebrate our friends, the saints. Mary has many feasts. On January 1, we celebrate the feast of Mary, Mother of God. Some other Mary feasts are the Annunciation (March 25), when the angel visited Mary, and the Immaculate Conception (December 8), when we remember that Mary was born free of all sin.

ANDRÉ BESSETTE

JANUARY 6

One nickel at a time...

What can you buy with a nickel? St. André Bessette turned some nickels into a beautiful place to pray. St. André knew that you don't have to be a big, important person to do great things.

St. André was a sickly orphan when he first came to the priests and brothers of the Holy Cross in Canada. He was sent to serve at a school, where he answered the door, cared for the sick, scrubbed floors, and took care of the gardens. People loved the gentle and happy brother and brought the sick to him for healing. Brother André said he didn't heal people; St. Joseph did. But he wanted to give people a place to pray that would also honor St. Joseph. So he started giving haircuts, charging five cents apiece. When he had saved $200 in nickels and other donations, he had a little shrine built. It was just one small room, but over time, Brother André's shrine grew into the largest Catholic church in Canada: St. Joseph's Oratory of Mount Royal. Millions of people pray and go to Mass there every year. And it all began with some nickels—and lots of prayers!

> **GOOD QUESTION!**
> Is there something small and good you might do today? (Who knows? It might turn into something big and great!)

Imagine your own place to pray

If you could create a place where people could come to pray, what would it be like? Use the space here to draw a prayer place of your own. **Use your imagination to make it the best it can be!**

GOOD to KNOW

Saint André never took credit for anything he did. He often said, "I have only my great devotion to Saint Joseph to guide me."

JOSEPHINE BAKHITA

FEBRUARY 8

"Love the Lord!"

It's hard to imagine how terrible St. Josephine Bakhita's childhood was. When she was about seven years old, she was kidnapped and sold as a slave in North Africa. She was so frightened, she couldn't even remember her name. So her kidnappers cruelly called her Bakhita, which means "fortunate," or "lucky."

A slave's life is the opposite of lucky and fortunate. Bakhita was mistreated and often beaten. She was never paid for her work. But things began to change when the family she served sent Bakhita with one of the children to a convent in Italy. The kind sisters shared Jesus' love with Bakhita. She asked to be baptized and took the name Josephine. When her owners sent for her, Josephine courageously refused to go. The sisters took her case to court, and Josephine was set free. Now she could do whatever she wanted. And Josephine wanted to serve God. She became a sister. You might think that after her horrible childhood, Josephine would be angry. Instead, she treated everyone with kindness and love. She said, "Be good, love the Lord, pray for those who do not know him. What a great grace it is to know God!"

> **GOOD QUESTION!**
> When you are treated badly, how do you respond? Ask Jesus to help you.

Feel Better

We've all had times when we've been hurt by others. How can you get from feeling bad to feeling better? Circle all the good ideas. **Draw an x through any ideas that won't help you.**

PRAY

TALK ABOUT IT

HOLD A GRUDGE

HELP OTHERS FEEL BETTER

FORGIVE

GOOD to KNOW

When someone asked what she would do if she ever met the people who had kidnapped her, St. Josephine answered, "I would kneel and kiss their hands. For if these things had not happened, I would not have been a Christian and a religious today."

JOSEPH

MARCH 19 (AND MAY 1)

Saint of action!

St. Joseph was sound asleep after a long day. Suddenly, an angel spoke to him in a dream and told him to get up. Now. "Take the child and his mother, flee to Egypt, and stay there until I tell you," the angel said. "Herod is going to search for the child to destroy him." Joseph didn't wait. He got up and took Mary and little baby Jesus to Egypt. Imagine what that must have been like! He didn't have time to prepare, or even say goodbye to anyone. Then, there was Egypt, a foreign land. People spoke a different language and worshiped strange gods. Joseph didn't know anyone there. How would he find work to support his family? But Joseph didn't let any of this stop him from doing what God wanted.

It isn't always easy to do what God wants. Sometimes people want us to do what they want. Sometimes we want to do what we want, and we turn away from God. When we're having trouble doing what God wants, we can remember St. Joseph. Make St. Joseph your friend and ask God for Joseph's strength, courage, and goodness.

> **GOOD QUESTION!**
> As you think of Joseph bringing his family to Egypt, think of any kids who are new at school or in your neighborhood. Do you think they are scared? How can you make them feel welcome?

Powerful Friends, Powerful Prayers

Remember St. André? He prayed to our friend St. Joseph for help. We call this type of prayer an **INTERCESSION**. That's a prayer that's said on behalf of someone else. We can ask the saints to pray to Jesus on our behalf. The prayers of the saints are powerful! But we can pray on behalf of others too. Who are some people you know who need God's help today? **Write their names here and pray for them this week!**

_____   _____

_____   _____

_____   _____

GOOD to KNOW

The Bible tells us about the good things St. Joseph did, but nothing about what he said. Pope Francis says, "Be like St. Joseph: a man of dreams, not a dreamer; a man of silence, because he respects God's plan."

BERNADETTE SOUBIROUS

APRIL 16

Saint of the sick

Imagine being so poor that the only place you can find to live is a drafty old jail. That's where Bernadette's family lived, in the little town of Lourdes, France. But that didn't keep God's love from Bernadette. He had something special planned for her. On a cold day in 1858, as she gathered firewood, Bernadette spotted a dazzling light in a little cave. A beautiful young woman appeared there. It was Mary! She smiled at Bernadette and prayed with her. When Bernadette tried to tell her family and friends about the girl, most people didn't believe her. Still, they followed her back to the cave to see what would happen. Mary appeared seventeen more times, and no one but Bernadette could see her. Mary told Bernadette that people needed to pray for sinners. Then she told Bernadette to drink and wash herself with water from the ground. Bernadette dug in the mud. People watching thought she was crazy. But slowly, water began to trickle up. Later, a woman with a diseased arm washed there and was instantly healed. Today, the waters at Lourdes still flow, bringing healing and hope to millions of people every year.

> **GOOD QUESTION!**
> Bernadette wasn't only poor, she suffered from diseases like cholera and asthma. Why do you think God chose her for this important message?

Saintly Code

You could say that the saints lived by a code. But it's not a secret code, it's simply a kind of code for living that Jesus gave us, called the Beatitudes. **Use the code below to learn one Beatitude that might describe St. Bernadette.**

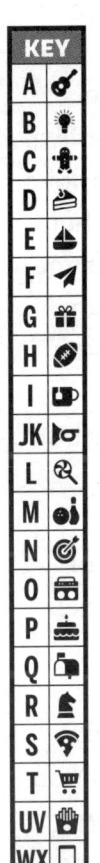

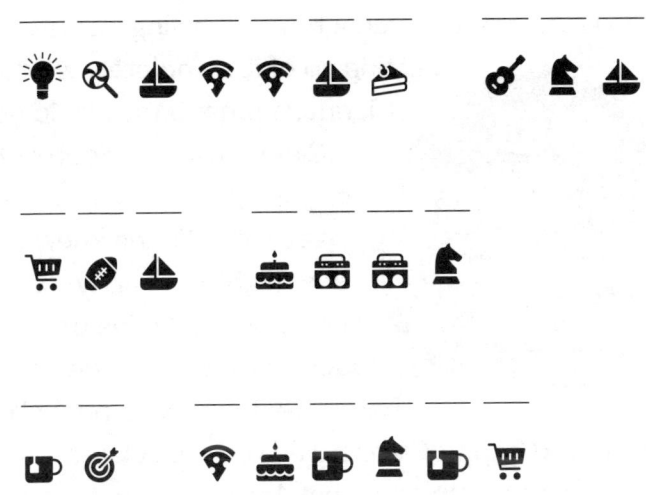

GOOD to KNOW

After the visions ended, Bernadette joined a convent where she worked with the sick until she became too sick herself. She suffered from tuberculosis, but said, "O Jesus, I no longer feel my cross when I think of yours."

GIANNA BERETTA MOLLA

APRIL 28

Mom, doctor, hero!

Gianna loved helping people, so she became a doctor. She loved her husband, Pietro, and their four children. Most of all, Gianna loved God. When she was pregnant with her fourth child, doctors discovered a tumor growing inside of her. Getting rid of it completely would save Gianna, but her baby would not survive. So Gianna told her doctors to remove only what they could and keep her baby safe. Gianna knew this meant she might not survive. But Gianna loved her baby. The operation was successful, and on the Saturday before Easter in 1962, her baby was born, healthy and happy. Gianna died one week later.

> **GOOD QUESTION!**
> How does Gianna's love for her child remind you of Jesus' love for all of us?

St. Gianna reminds us that Jesus calls us to love everyone—not just the people we can see right in front of us. We are called to love children and babies who are sick, and families who can't get enough food. We are called to love elderly people in nursing homes and people without any homes at all. Today, pray for someone you don't know. Maybe someone in another country who is suffering. Maybe someone who hasn't been born yet. You might not know their names, but God does. And God loves them, just as he loves you.

Who do we love?

Finish the Bible quotes to know!

DOWN

1 ...the love of God has been poured out into our hearts through the holy __ that has been given to us. (Romans 5:5)

2 You shall love your __ as yourself. (Matthew 22:39)

3 For God so loved the __ that he gave his only Son... (John 3:16)

5 ...love your __, do good to those who hate you... (Luke 6:27)

ACROSS

4 This is how all will know that you are my __, if you have love for one another. (John 13:35)

6 See what love the Father has bestowed on us that we may be called the __ of God.

7 Love the __, your God, with all your heart...soul, and...mind. (Matthew 22:37)

8 We love because he __ loved us. (1 John 4:19)

JOAN OF ARC

MAY 30

"God is with me."

Joan began hearing saints speak when she was about twelve. At first, they told her to love Jesus, be good, and go to Mass. Later, they told her to save her country. Joan lived in France. At the time, the country was torn apart by war. Joan trusted God and did what the voices told her. She went to the prince and convinced him to let her lead an army!

Joan wasn't like other leaders. She was a teenager who couldn't read or write. She had letters sent to the enemy, warning them to leave the country peacefully, because the "King of Heaven wills it." When they refused, Joan led her soldiers into battle and won victory after victory. Joan also spent time in prayer. She reminded her soldiers to go to Mass and receive the sacraments.

In 1430, Joan was captured by her enemies and put in prison. In an unjust trial, people made up lies about her. Joan was condemned to die a horrible death: burning at the stake. Joan begged to look at a crucifix as she died, saying, "I am not afraid because God is with me. I was born to do this."

GOOD QUESTION!
Things happen in our lives that we don't always understand. How can we know God is with us at those times?

What does the Bible Say?

Joan trusted in God, just as the Bible tells us. **Finish the Bible quote below by placing the correct words in the spaces.**

Have no _ _ _ _ _ T _ at all, but in everything, by _ R _ _ _ _ _ and petition, with thanksgiving, make your _ _ _ U _ _ _ _ known to God. Then the peace of God that S _ _ _ _ _ _ _ _ _ all understanding will guard your _ _ _ _ T _ and minds in Christ Jesus. [PHILIPPIANS 4:6]

PRAYER
HEARTS
REQUESTS
ANXIETY
SURPASSES

GOOD to KNOW

After her death, Joan was declared a **MARTYR**. That's someone who refuses to give up their faith, even in death. Joan of Arc is the **PATRON SAINT** of France.

ANTHONY OF PADUA

JUNE 13

Always guiding us to Jesus

Every time Anthony decided to do something, God had a different plan. Anthony wanted to be a missionary, but when he arrived in Africa, he became so sick he was sent home. Sailing back to Portugal, a storm blew his ship off course, and he wound up in Sicily, near Italy. Anthony went to a monastery where he thought he'd live a quiet life. One day at Mass, someone asked Anthony to give the homily. Anthony hadn't prepared anything, but he gave such a stirring talk that soon people were begging him to give more talks. So much for his quiet life!

Most people know St. Anthony as the saint to turn to when you've lost something. It probably comes from a famous story about a young friar who decided to leave the community where Anthony lived. The friar took Anthony's most prized book with him. Anthony thought he'd misplaced the book and didn't realize it had been taken. As he prayed to Jesus for the book's return, the friar had a change of heart. He returned and confessed to Anthony that he'd taken the book. Once again, God had a bigger plan and returned something more important than a book—a lost soul!

> **GOOD QUESTION!**
> Have you ever planned something that turned out differently from what you expected? How can you see God's work there?

Help Bobby find his missing book!

Saint Anthony is the patron saint of lost things. But Like Saint Anthony, we can help others find things. **Can you help Bobby find his lost book?**

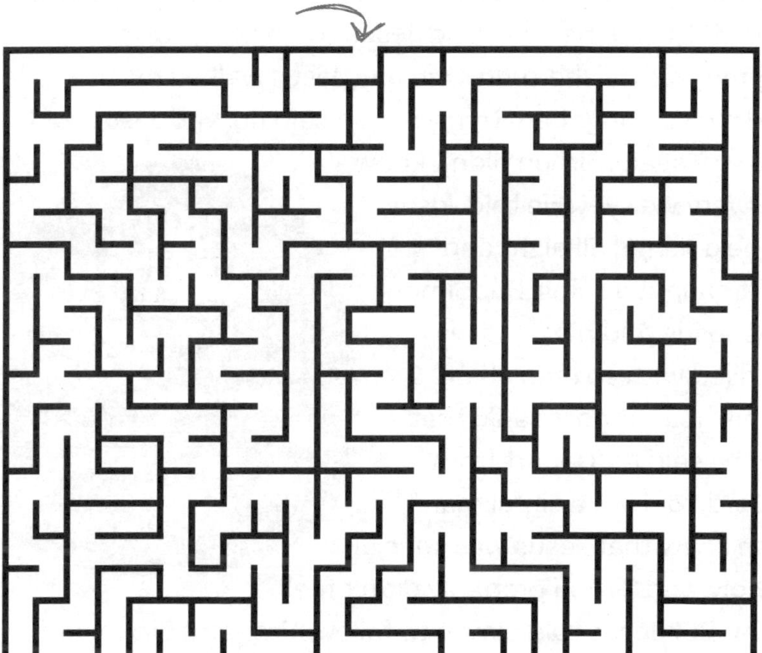

GOOD to KNOW

Saint Anthony was a good friend of Saint Francis of Assisi—we'll learn more about him **later!**

PETER

JUNE 29

Saint Peter's rocky start

Have you ever said something and then wished you hadn't? Simon did. Once he even told Jesus to go away! Oops!

Simon was a fisherman. One day, Jesus walked by and asked if he'd caught anything. Simon said no, and Jesus told him to try again. Simon didn't know Jesus very well yet. He told Jesus that he'd fished all night and hadn't caught a thing. But Simon did as Jesus told him, and his nets filled with so many fish that his boat almost sank. That's when he said it: "Depart from me, Lord, for I am a sinful man." Simon knew that Jesus was special and holy, and Simon probably didn't feel worthy. But Jesus told Simon to follow him—and Simon did. Jesus changed Simon's name to Cephas, which means "rock." We know him as Peter, the leader of Jesus' Apostles. Peter was there during Jesus' biggest moments, like the Transfiguration and the Last Supper. Peter was also nearby at Jesus' trial. But Peter probably wished he'd kept quiet again, because he denied Jesus three times. He felt so awful that he went out and wept. Still, the risen Jesus forgave Peter, and even gave him the job of leading his whole church!

> **GOOD QUESTION!**
> Peter made some mistakes. But Jesus saw more than mistakes. He loved Peter. Knowing this, what do you think are some good things Jesus sees in you?

Saint Peter and you

Did you know that God gives you the same gifts he gave to St. Peter, and to all his saints? They are the gifts of the Holy Spirit, and you receive them at your baptism, your confirmation, and every time you receive Jesus in the Eucharist. Read about them here.
Then find them in the puzzle.

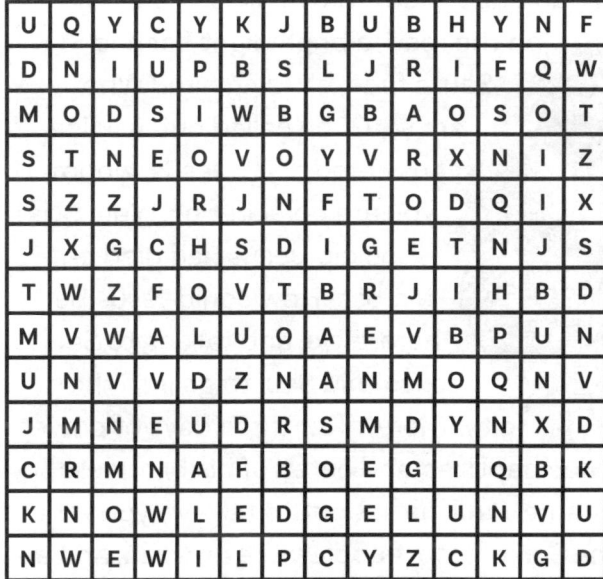

Wisdom helps us see things as God sees them.

Understanding helps us see the truth of what God says.

Knowledge is how we explore all that God has revealed.

Counsel helps us make choices to follow God's plan.

Fortitude is the courage to do what is right.

Piety helps us pray in love and thankfulness.

Wonder and Awe means doing all we can to stay in the power of God's love.

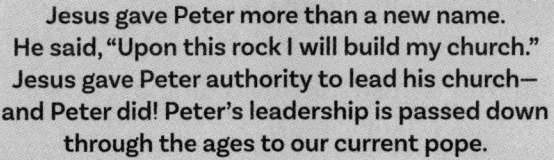

GOOD to KNOW

Jesus gave Peter more than a new name. He said, "Upon this rock I will build my church." Jesus gave Peter authority to lead his church—and Peter did! Peter's leadership is passed down through the ages to our current pope.

PAUL

JUNE 29

Change of heart

After the risen Jesus went to heaven, his followers spread the good news of his saving power and love. A man named Saul didn't like that idea. He chased down Jesus' followers, put them in chains, and had them thrown in jail. One day on the road, a bright light flashed in Saul's face, blinding him. "Who are you?" he called out. A voice answered, "I am Jesus, whom you are persecuting." Saul was shocked. Jesus had died on a cross! How could Jesus be here, alive, and talking to Saul? Jesus told Saul to go into the city. There, after three days of prayer and fasting, Saul was baptized and cured of his blindness. Using his Roman name, Paul, he set out to tell everyone that Jesus truly was the Son of God. People were amazed, and a little afraid. Wasn't this the man who had been persecuting Jesus' followers? But that didn't stop Paul. He traveled all over, preaching about Jesus and helping the new Christian communities. He was thrown in jail, just as he had once done to Jesus' followers. How did he do so much good after doing so much bad? The answer is Jesus. Jesus didn't just change Paul's mind. Jesus changed Paul's heart.

> **GOOD QUESTION!**
> Is there something you want to change for the better in your life? Who can you ask for help?

Words in words

Turning to God with your whole heart like St. Paul did is called conversion. We may not be throwing people in jail the way St. Paul did, but we all turn away from God—whenever we sin. God's heart is so full of love for us, he is always calling us to conversion.

Conversion is a word that's full of other smaller words, like cover and sir. There are at least 25 more.
Fill up the heart with all the conversion words you can find.

CONVERSION

GOOD to KNOW

St. Paul wrote a large part of the Bible; he wrote many of the letters we read in the New Testament. He even wrote some letters while he was in prison!

TERESA OF CALCUTTA

SEPTEMBER 5

Bringing Jesus' light and love to everyone

Remember how Jesus spoke to Paul? St. Teresa heard Jesus speaking to her too. But instead of shining a bright light, Jesus said, "Come be my light."

Teresa was born about 2,000 years after St. Paul, in a city called Skopje, in Southeastern Europe. She felt called to follow Jesus, and she became a sister, serving as a teacher in India. But when Jesus spoke to her, she said it was a "call within a call." Teresa had always said she would never refuse anything Jesus asked of her. And now Jesus was asking her to serve him as a light to the world. Teresa went into the streets of India, to bring Jesus' light and love to those who were in the darkest places of their lives: the poorest of the poor, the suffering and dying. Mother Teresa, as she was called, lived among the poor and served them. Soon, others joined her. She called her sisters the Missionaries of Charity. Their job, Mother Teresa said, was to care for "the hungry, the naked, the homeless, the crippled, the blind, the lepers, all those people who feel unwanted, unloved, uncared for."

> **GOOD QUESTION!**
> Think about these words of Jesus: "I was hungry and you gave me food, I was thirsty and you gave me drink, a stranger and you welcomed me, naked and you clothed me, ill and you cared for me, in prison and you visited me" (Matthew 25:35-36). What is Jesus saying to you?

St. Teresa's words of wisdom

St Teresa said many inspiring things. **Finish the quotes by unscrambling the letters.** Think about St. Teresa's words and what they mean to you.

I can do things you cannot, you can do things I cannot; _____ [regettho] we can do great things.

Let no one ever come to you without leaving better and _____ [pparhie]. Be the living expression of God's kindness: kindness in your face, kindness in your eyes, kindness in your _____ [lmise].

Not all of us can do great things. But we can do small things with great _____ [vleo].

GOOD to KNOW

St. Teresa felt that the worst poverty in the world was feeling lonely and unloved. She made it her goal to serve people in joy. She said, "If we went to them with a sad face, we would only make them much more depressed."

THÉRÈSE OF LISIEUX

OCTOBER 1

A little flower in God's garden

Do you ever wish you were smarter, stronger, more athletic, or just...someone else? St. Thérèse of Lisieux wants you to know how much God loves you exactly as you are!

Thérèse lived as a cloistered sister. That means she didn't leave the convent where she lived. Her days were filled with prayer and hard, sometimes dull, work. Thérèse often fell asleep when she was supposed to be praying. At first, she felt terrible for being so weak, but then Thérèse remembered that parents don't stop loving their children just because they're asleep. She knew God loved her at every moment—even if she couldn't stay awake to love him back!

Thérèse explained that we are all like different flowers in God's great garden of souls. She said God created small, quiet daisies and violets to grow next to big beautiful roses and showy white lilies. Thérèse imagined God walking in his garden of souls. Even the tiniest flowers, like Thérèse herself, were "destined to give joy to God's glances when he looks down at his feet." Perfection, she said, means "doing God's will and being what he wills us to be." You get closer to being a saint when you work on being the wonderful person God created you to be!

> **GOOD QUESTION!**
> How do you feel when you pray? Can you be completely yourself—the person God loves?

Saint Thérèse is working hard for you in heaven!

Saint Thérèse said, "I want to spend my heaven doing good on earth." Thérèse is part of the Communion of Saints. Those are all the baptized people in heaven and on earth, who are part of God's family. You're a part of the Communion of Saints too! You have saints like Thérèse in heaven, working hard for you. How can you pass this good on to others? **Write down one good thing you will do every day this week for the people you love.**

1. _____
2. _____
3. _____
4. _____
5. _____
6. _____
7. _____

GOOD to KNOW

Thérèse's superior at the convent asked her to keep a journal. It was later turned into a book called *The Story of a Soul*. People all over the world still read this book, in which Thérèse talks about living a simple life of love and joy. Thérèse called this her "little way."

FRANCIS OF ASSISI

OCTOBER 4

Francis finds a treasure

We've met saints who did as God asked. But did any of them ever misunderstand God's message? Francis was praying in an old church when he heard Jesus say, "Francis, repair my church which, as you see, is in ruins." Francis set out to fix the crumbling old church. Before long, though, he realized that Jesus had more in mind for him. Francis didn't have much of a plan, but he knew what Jesus had said in the gospels: "Go, sell what you have and give to the poor, and you will have treasure in heaven. Then come, follow me" (Matthew 19:21). Francis realized that this was what Jesus meant for him: to live a life of love and complete trust in God. So Francis gave away everything he had. Wearing rags and no shoes, Francis preached, cared for the poor and sick, and prayed. With no worldly goods to worry about, Francis felt truly free and full of God's joy. He celebrated God's creation all around him. Some people said he was crazy. Others joined him. They became known as Franciscans. Today, Franciscan friars, brothers, sisters, and laypeople all over the world continue Francis' way of life. They live in generosity. They see God's goodness everywhere and seek to share God's love with everyone.

> **GOOD QUESTION!**
> How can you see God's goodness and love in the people and things around you?

God's Creation Bingo

St. Francis saw God's love in everything God created. If the weather is nice, go outside and see how many of these gifts God has created for you. (If you can't go outside, see how many you can spot from inside: from your window, in books, or even around the house!) Some of the squares are free. **Be sure to do what they say!**

GOOD to KNOW

Saint Francis wrote a prayer song, *Canticle of the Sun*, which praises God for all he has created, such as "Brother Sun" and "Sister Moon."

JOHN XXIII

OCTOBER 11

Saint of ideas...and jokes

Do you like to have friends around who make you laugh? Then you might like to hang around St. John XXIII. He was a pope who liked to laugh and joke. Once, someone asked him how many people worked at the Vatican. He cracked, "About half of them." He also used to say, "Sometimes I wake up at night and think about some serious problem and think I must talk to the pope about it. Then the next day when I wake up, I remember that I am the pope."

Good Pope John, as he was called, also knew when it was time to be serious. Once when he was praying, he said, an idea came to him, "like a flash of heavenly light." He called for a historic meeting of thousands of church leaders to gather in Rome to pray, talk, debate, and come to some agreements about how the Catholic Church would help people in our modern world. The meeting, known as the Second Vatican Council, or Vatican II, helped Catholics understand more clearly that the church is the body of Christ and that we are all one with Christ. Our baptism calls each of us to be holy, following Christ just as the saints did.

> **GOOD QUESTION!**
> What is one thing you've learned from the saints about following Christ? What does this mean for you in your life?

Pick a Partner!

Even before he became pope, Saint John XXIII thought of the saints as friends. He especially admired Saint Charles Borromeo and Saint Francis de Sales. Have you chosen any saints to be friends?
Write about one saint you admire right here.

My Friend, Saint _____

Here's what I know about my friend

_____
_____

Here's more I'd like to know

_____
_____

Here's why this saint is my friend

_____
_____

Here are some ways I can be like my friend

_____
_____

GOOD to KNOW

Popes choose papal names when they are elected. Angelo Roncalli was the 23rd pope to choose the name John, becoming John XXIII.

JUAN DIEGO

DECEMBER 9

Loving Son

Juan Diego was worried. The beautiful lady he had met on the hilltop had told him that today she would give him something special. Something that would prove to the bishop that her request to build a church was real. But Juan Diego's uncle was sick, and maybe dying. He felt terrible about missing his meeting with the lady, but he had to find a doctor. On the way, he spotted her. She gently asked what was wrong and Juan Diego told her about his uncle. The lady (who you've probably guessed was Mary) said, "My dearest Juan Diego, am I not here, I who am your mother?" She promised Juan Diego that his uncle would be cured and told him to collect the flowers growing on the hill. Juan Diego trusted Mary. He brought the flowers to her and she arranged them in his tilma, or cloak. Mary told Juan Diego to take them to the bishop. When Juan Diego arrived at the bishop's house, he opened his tilma and the flowers spilled out. Even more amazing, a beautiful image appeared on the tilma. We know her as Our Lady of Guadalupe. To Juan Diego, she was a loving mother. And of course she was right—Juan Diego's uncle was cured!

> **GOOD QUESTION!**
> Imagine Mary asking you to tell your bishop that she wants a church built! What would you do? (Hint: read the story on page 2 about another heavenly visitor!)

Hidden Saints!

The Church gives people like Juan Diego the title of saint because of the holy, faithful lives they lived. (People in the process of being named saints are called blesseds.) Many people in heaven don't have this formal title, but they're still saints! **Now, can you find all the saints we've learned about here?** (Look for the names in **bold**.)

X	J	H	F	A	M	A	R	Y	E	P	Y	E	E	P
C	T	O	D	R	Z	N	H	L	B	E	T	G	A	J
H	A	I	H	N	A	J	O	C	Z	T	C	U	F	G
T	E	H	O	N	P	N	D	Q	E	E	L	Z	I	N
W	E	Q	S	D	X	D	C	D	D	R	O	A	J	E
O	H	R	C	L	A	X	A	I	P	I	N	L	O	Q
H	V	B	E	V	B	N	I	N	S	N	O	X	S	Z
J	A	W	Y	S	R	V	D	I	A	O	P	Z	E	X
P	H	O	N	E	A	N	K	N	I	I	H	Y	P	E
F	B	W	B	J	O	A	N	O	F	A	R	C	H	S
Y	N	O	H	T	N	A	J	O	S	E	P	H	I	E
Y	A	T	N	A	C	D	Q	Q	T	U	F	P	N	R
B	R	W	J	U	A	N	D	I	E	G	O	I	E	E
U	T	L	Q	I	W	F	F	A	F	O	H	T	M	H
Q	T	L	J	C	E	R	D	N	A	Q	Y	X	U	T

André Bessette
Anthony of Padua
Bernadette
Francis of Assisi
Gianna Beretta Molla
Joan of Arc
John XXIII
Joseph
Josephine Bakhita
Juan Diego
Mary
Paul
Peter
Teresa of Calcutta
Thérèse of Lisieux

GOOD to KNOW

In the Basilica of Our Lady of Guadalupe in Mexico City, you can still see Juan Diego's *tilma* with the beautiful image of Mary.

ALSO BY CONNIE CLARK

Fun Faith Activities for Summer

This thoroughly Catholic summer activity book makes a perfect year-end gift for families in Catholic schools and parish programs. With puzzles, games, and activities, it's bursting with fun facts, Bible verses, and prayers. Each page covers themes like summer sports and foods, Mary, the Mass, and much more.

32 PAGES | $2.95* | 5½" X 8½"
9781627850100

Fun Prayer Activities for Summer

This prayer-themed activity booklet can help parishes and schools extend faith formation over the summer, and help parents feel good about giving their children activities to feed their faith. Puzzles, games, and activities for ages 6-11 teach about general prayers of praise, thanksgiving, and sorrow for sins, plus specific devotions like pilgrimages and novenas. This engaging booklet shows that prayer isn't just for school or church—it's for any season and any time, day or night.

32 PAGES | $2.95* | 5½" X 8½"
9781627850742

*BOOKLET PRICING
100+ copies...$1.95 each • **50–99** copies...$2.45 each • **1–49** copies...$2.95 each

TO ORDER CALL 1-800-321-0411
OR VISIT WWW.TWENTYTHIRDPUBLICATIONS.COM

TWENTY-THIRD PUBLICATIONS
A division of Bayard, Inc.